The Beginner's Guide to
BRAIDING
The craft of Kumihimo

I would like to thank my family and the staff at Search Press for their help in making this book, and all those who have inspired and encouraged me along the way.

The Beginner's Guide to
BRAIDING

The craft of Kumihimo

JACQUI CAREY

SEARCH PRESS

First published in Great Britain 1997
Search Press Limited
Wellwood, North Farm Road,
Tunbridge Wells, Kent TN2 3DR

Reprinted 1998, 2000, 2002, 2004, 2006

ISBN 0 85532 828 2

Suppliers

If you have any difficulty in obtaining any of
the materials and equipment mentioned in this
book, then please write for further information,
either to the publishers,

Search Press Limited, Wellwood,
North Farm Road, Tunbridge Wells,
Kent TN2 3DR, England,

or to the author, Jacqui Carey,

Carey Company, 75, Slade Close,
Ottery St. Mary, Devon EX11 1SY, England.

Printed in Malaysia by Times Offset (M) Sdn Bhd

CONTENTS

INTRODUCTION

Kumihimo is the ancient art of Japanese braidmaking. The craft covers a wide range of techniques made on various types of equipment. This book looks at braiding on a *marudai* (round stand), which is the most popular and versatile piece of equipment in use today.

Working with a traditional marudai is a delightful experience. This piece of equipment is aesthetic in appearance, feel and sound, and the gentle rhythm of the repeated moves has a soothing quality. Easy-to-make alternative equipment makes Kumihimo an accessible craft and allows anyone to have a go. This book sets out to demonstrate that Kumihimo does not have to be complicated to be beautiful. Kumihimo braids are often made with many bobbins following complex sets of moves. Yet simple sequences can provide an array of stunning results. In this book, just six sets of moves are shown, each one creating a distinct type of braid. From these basic moves, countless variations can be created by using different combinations of colour, texture and material.

Throughout history, Kumihimo has been admired for its dual qualities of usefulness and beauty. Braids have been used in all walks of life but they are mainly associated with the Samurai who used them extensively in the construction of their armour. As well as being highly decorative, silk braids had the strength and flexibility needed to lace the lamellar sections of the armour.

When the Samurai class was abolished at the end of the nineteenth century, the focus of Kumihimo shifted to fashion. *Haori* jackets were fastened with two short braids tied with a choice of knots. The small loop at the end of each braid enabled the ties to be interchangeable, depending on the occasion. Kumihimo was also used as an *obi-jime*, a cord secured around the fabric sash of a kimono. This fashion created an alternative use for the sword and helmet braids, and it remains the most common application of Kumihimo today.

Modern obi-jime.

Above and below:
Modern 'haori' ties.

Left:
Samurai throat guard (nodawa) dating from the Edo period. Silk braids, in a range of colours and designs, lace together the sections of lacquered scales. Braid is also used as a tie for attaching the guard around the neck and as a decorative 'agemaki' knot at the centre.
Courtesy of the Anderson Collection.

MATERIALS AND EQUIPMENT

Choice of warp threads

A warp is the collection of threads used to make a braid. Traditionally, Kumihimo warps are made from smooth, lustrous silk, although today, a silk substitute known as 'biron' is also used. Both fibres are available in standard pre-made ropes intended for the production of *obi-jime*. Ropes are 2.7m (9ft) long and consist of strands lightly twisted together; silk rope has forty-two strands and biron has thirty-nine strands. Silk has a three-ply structure and weighs 22g/1000m (¾oz/1000yd). In this book, references within warp details of half-rope thickness have nominally twenty strands.

It is possible to use practically any thread or fibre for braiding; generally, smooth, shiny threads create a better defined result, but textural threads or combinations of textures can produce some stunning effects.

The surface pattern on a braid is produced through the use of colour. The combination of colours, their ratio to one another and their starting positions all help to make new pattern possibilities. Strong colour contrasts provide well-defined patterns, whereas close tonal blends create more subtle designs.

It is possible to create a myriad of different braids from just one sequence of moves by altering the colour, thread type, thickness and texture. The thickness of a braid is determined by the number and thickness of threads used on each bobbin.

The length of finished braid will vary depending on the braidmaker, the type of threads and the counterbalance weight. As a rough guide, start with a set of threads twice the length of the required braid. It is difficult to join threads neatly while working, so it is best to start braiding with a little more length than you think you will need.

Marudai

The traditional marudai is made from smooth, close-grained wood, with the top surface, the *kagami* or mirror, supported by four legs fixed to a base plate.

The mirror is the most important feature of a marudai. The surface and all edges must be perfectly smooth so that the threads can flow over them without snagging.

Marudais are available in several sizes, but one with a 25cm (10in) diameter mirror is a good average.

Marudais are also available in other materials, such as clear acrylic, which allows the braid to be viewed while work is in progress. Alternatively, you can make a simple marudai by taping a circle of card to the top of a lampshade frame.

A traditional wooden marudai showing work in progress.

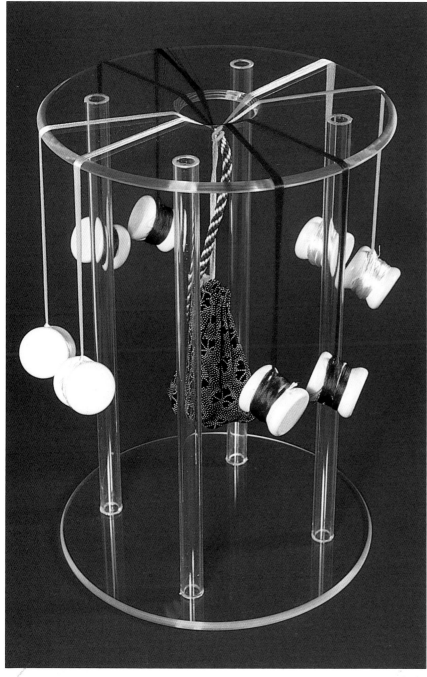

A clear acrylic marudai with plastic bobbins.

A home-made marudai using a cardboard mirror attached to a lampshade frame. The bobbins are also home-made from photographic film canisters.

Bobbins

As with the marudai, traditional bobbins are made from wood but you can also buy plastic ones or even make your own. Wooden and plastic bobbins come in a variety of different standard weights. However, when making a braid, a set of bobbins of equal weight must be used so as to provide an even tension on the threads. Lighter bobbins are used for making finer braids and heavier bobbins for thicker braids. The most common weights are 70g (2½oz) and 100g (3½oz) bobbins, although other weights, such as 37g (1¼oz) and 240g (8½oz) are also available.

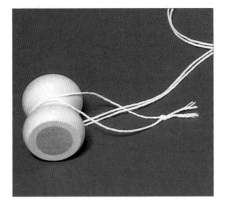

Traditional wooden bobbin
Attached to each bobbin is a cotton leader, approximately 40cm (16in) in length. Its purpose is to prevent wastage by allowing the bobbin to hang at the correct height while the end of the warp is braided.

Home-made bobbins
You can make your own bobbins from photographic film canisters filled with weights or small coins. Attach elastic bands to each side of the canister to prevent the threads from slipping off.

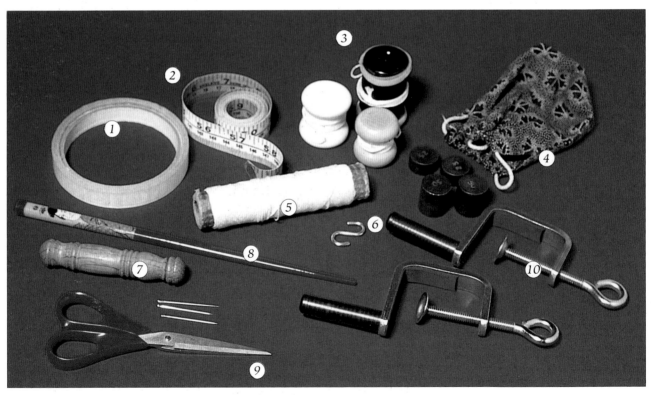

1. Sticky tape
2. Tape measure
3. Bobbins: a traditional wooden bobbin, an acrylic plastic one and a home-made one
4. Drawstring weight bag and an assortment of weights
5. Soft cotton
6. S-hook
7. Needles and case
8. Chopstick
9. Scissors
10. Warping posts

Counterbalance weights

To offset the bobbin weight, and to provide the correct tension in the braid, a counterbalance weight is attached to the end of the threads. These weights are usually held in a drawstring bag attached to the end of the warp.

Throughout this book there are details of the bobbin and counterbalance weights used to make the braids illustrated. As a rough guide, the counterbalance weight should be half the combined weight of the bobbins.

It is worth remembering that the more weight, the looser and softer the braid. The less weight, the tighter and more compact the braid.

You may want to experiment with the counterbalance weight to best fit in with your technique, your chosen thread type, the bobbin size and desired effect.

Warping posts

Warps are wound around two posts. Clamp-type posts that fix to a tabletop work best, but you can use any form of post provided that at least one is adjustable so you can vary the distance between the posts.

Other equipment

A smooth chopstick or knitting needle is used to secure the warp threads under the mirror when braiding is not in progress.

A small, metal S-hook is used to attach the weight bag to the beginning of the warp.

You will also need some sewing needles, a tape measure, a pair of scissors and some sticky tape.

Working the braids

It is important to be comfortable and relaxed whilst braiding. Kneeling is the traditional working position for Kumihimo, but it is not suitable for everyone. An alternative is to raise the marudai so that you can sit or stand as you work.

Braids are created by moving pairs of warp threads simultaneously to new positions on the mirror.

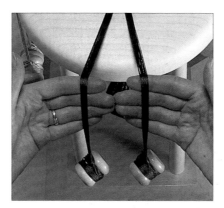

When moving warp threads, lift them – not the bobbins – from a point between the bobbin and the surface of the mirror. Try to make the movements as even as possible, allowing the threads to flow across the fingers. Do not grip the threads between fingers and thumbs.

Each sequence of moves produces a unique structure of braid. However, different patterns can be created on the same braid by rearranging the starting positions of the coloured threads, and you can use the same set of moves with different warps. At the end of each project there is a selection of braids that can be made with the same set of moves, together with warp details and a start position diagram.

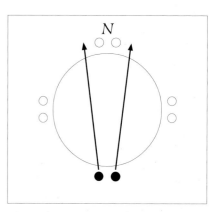

Throughout this book, diagrams like this show the movement of the bobbins. The large circle represents the mirror which is divided into four compass points, with south nearest to the braider. The small circles represent the warp bobbins, and the arrows show the movement of bobbins. Similar diagrams without the arrows are also used to show the initial arrangement of colours.

When working with many strands of thread on one bobbin, it is possible to have the threads lying parallel or twisted. It is suggested that they remain parallel unless otherwise stated. An anti-clockwise twist on the threads is referred to as a Z-twist and a clockwise one as an S-twist.

SQUARE BRAID

This first project shows you, stage by stage, how to make a braid that has a square cross-section. Using the materials listed and the colour arrangement shown in the warp details box below, a soft, chunky braid with a stripe of colour on each face of the square is produced. The finished braid will be about 55cm (22in) long with tassels at each end.

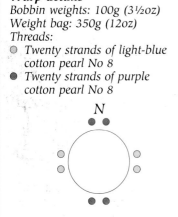

Warp details
Bobbin weights: 100g (3½oz)
Weight bag: 350g (12oz)
Threads:
- *Twenty strands of light-blue cotton pearl No 8*
- *Twenty strands of purple cotton pearl No 8*

Winding a warp

The warp is a collection of threads used to make a braid; all the braids in this book are made with warps with eight sets of threads. There are different ways of making a warp, and here is a way of making a warp from balls of embroidery thread. Making a warp from traditional, ready-made biron ropes, is shown on pages 28–9.

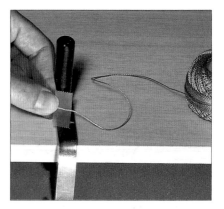

1 Set the warp posts 1m (40in) apart and attach the end of the thread to the left-hand post with a piece of sticky tape.

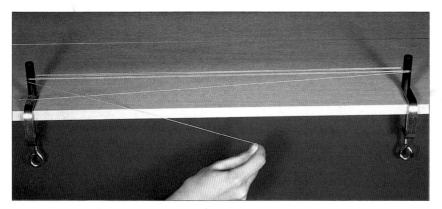

2 Take the thread round the right-hand post and make a mental count of one. Wind the thread back to the left-hand post and make a count of two. Continue winding and counting until you reach twenty.

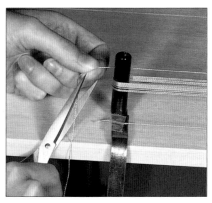

3 At the left-hand post, hold the thread to retain tension and cut off the free end.

Joining warp threads to bobbin leaders

Lift all the threads off the left-hand post only and attach this free end to the bobbin leader as shown. The traditional Japanese 'attaching' knot needs a little practice, but it is very secure when in place. It is helpful to keep the threads taut throughout the knotting sequence. If you have difficulty tying this traditional knot, you can use other knots, such as the reef knot shown below.

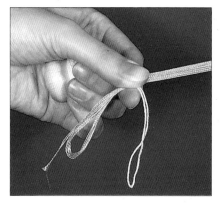

1 Hold the bobbin in the palm of one hand and pinch the leader between thumb and index finger. Now lay the warp under the leader and hold in place.

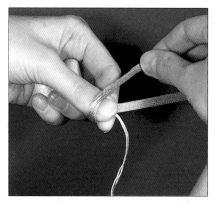

2 Using your other hand, fold the end of the warp threads over the top of your thumb.

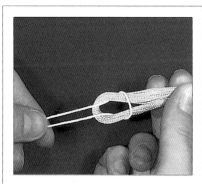

A reef knot tied through the leader loop can be used as an alternative to the traditional Japanese attaching knot.

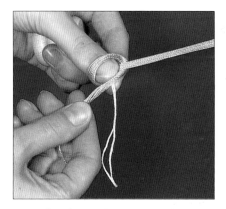

3 Take the ends round behind the warp threads, back over the leader and hold in place under your thumb.

4 Still pinching the leader and warp threads, slide the loops off the thumb and lay them flat over the leader.

5 Pull part of the leader up through the loops.

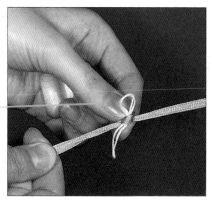

6 Finally, pull hard on the end of the warp threads to tighten the knot round the leader.

Winding the bobbins and making the slip knot

With the cotton threads still hanging from the right-hand warping post, and keeping the threads taut, roll the leader and warp threads smoothly on to the bobbin. Stop winding when the bobbin is about 40cm (16in) from the warping post. Next, tie a slip knot in the warp threads as shown, to stop them un-winding. Again, keep the warp threads taut while the knot is made.

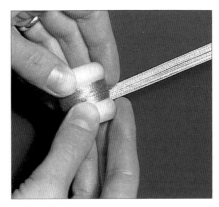

1 Hold the bobbin so that the warp threads are underneath.

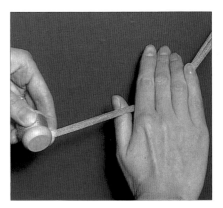

2 Place the palm of your right hand on top of the threads and tuck your thumb under them.

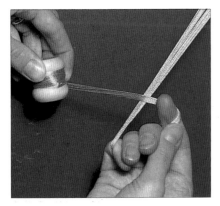

3 Twist your right hand so that the warp threads make a loop around your fingers.

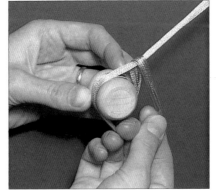

4 Bring the bobbin into the loop from underneath and arrange the loop round the centre of the bobbin.

5 Slide the bobbin down to tighten the slip knot and leave it hanging from the right-hand warping post.

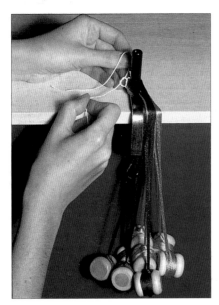

6 Wind the other bobbins in the same way until you have four bobbins wound with light-blue cotton pearl and four with purple cotton pearl. With all eight bobbins still hanging from the right-hand warping post, take a length of thread through all of the loops on the post and tie them together with a reef knot.

7 Tie a second knot a short distance from the first to create a loop as shown. This will be used for attaching the S-hook.

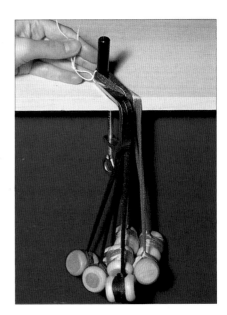

Mounting the warp on the marudai

When all eight sets of threads have been tied together, they must be placed on the marudai, connected to the counterbalance weight bag and arranged round the mirror, ready to start braiding.

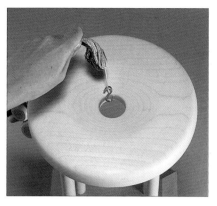

1 Attach the S-hook into the loop in the end of the warp and pass it through the hole in the mirror.

2 Attach the weight bag to the other end of the S-hook.

3 Arrange the threads round the surface of the mirror. Place pairs of purple threads at the north and south positions and pairs of light-blue ones at the east and west positions. Do not worry if you have to cross over the threads in the centre.

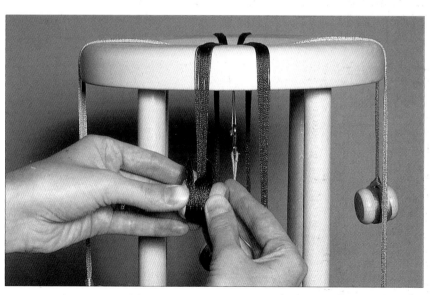

4 Adjust the bobbins until they are all about 15cm (6in) below the surface of the mirror. Lower a bobbin by rolling it away from the loop of the slip knot. Raise it by removing the slip knot, winding up the bobbin and re-tying the knot.

Working the braid

This square braid is made by repeating a sequence of four movements. The sequence can be used with a variety of colour arrangements, so try to memorise it as a set of positional moves rather than colour moves.

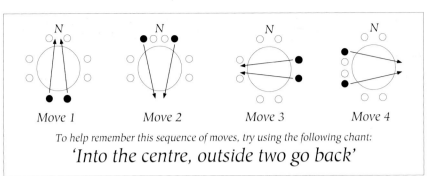

Move 1   *Move 2*   *Move 3*   *Move 4*

To help remember this sequence of moves, try using the following chant:

'Into the centre, outside two go back'

1 Lift the two sets of threads at the south . . .

. . . and place them down between those at the north.

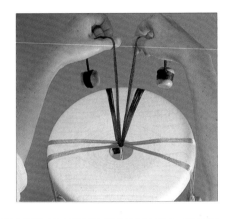

2 Lift the outer two sets of threads at the north . . .

. . . and place them down at the south.

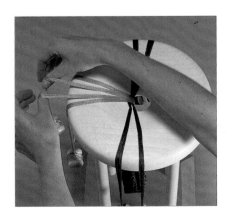

3 Lift the two sets of threads at the east . . .

. . . and place them down between those at the west.

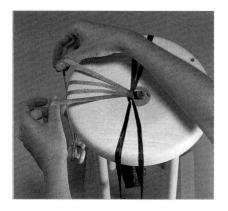

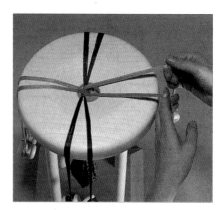

4 Lift the outer two sets of threads at the west . . .

. . . and place them down at the east.

Points of braiding

The point of braiding is at the centre of the marudai where the threads come together. The configuration of threads at this point changes with each of the four moves. This can be a vital reference to let you know where you are in the sequence, and so rectify errors should they occur.

Ready to start move 1. The bobbins are distributed evenly round the marudai and the point of braiding is central. Note that east and west threads are on top.

Ready to start move 2. The uneven distribution of the bobbins offsets the point of braiding to the north.

Ready to start move 3. The bobbins are distributed evenly and the point of braiding is central. Note that the north and south threads are on top.

Ready to start move 4. The uneven distribution of the bobbins offsets the point of braiding to the west.

Adjusting the weight bag

As braiding progresses, the bobbins rise up and the counter-balance weight sinks down. You must readjust the positions of the bobbins and the weight bag frequently. Adjust the bobbins as shown on page 17, and the weight bag as shown here. At the first adjustment, the S-hook is discarded and the weight bag is attached to the braid with a lark's-head knot.

1 Slide a chopstick between the warp threads, above the point of braiding but below the mirror.

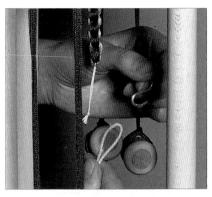

2 Remove the weight bag and the S-hook from the end of the braid.

3 Place your thumb and index finger inside the drawstring of the weight bag...

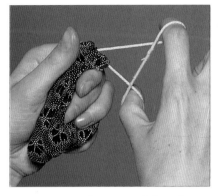

... turn your finger and thumb around the outside of the drawstring to make two loops...

... and bring the two loops together to complete the lark's-head knot.

4 Pass the end of the braid through the lark's-head knot and pull the knot tight.

5 As the braid gets longer, slide the lark's-head knot further up the braid.

Tip
Always insert a chopstick between the warp threads when adjusting the counterbalance weight, and whenever you take a break during braiding.

Finishing

The cotton leaders attached to the warp threads make it possible to braid right up to the end of the threads. However, be careful not to snag the attaching knots as they cross the mirror. Do not worry if you end up with uneven lengths of warp threads – this is due to uneven braiding movement, and will improve with practice. Before removing the leaders, tie a temporary securing knot over the end of the braid to stop it unravelling.

1 Stop braiding when the ends of the warp threads are quite short.

2 Tie a securing knot round the braid with soft thread and slide it up close to the point of braiding before tightening it.

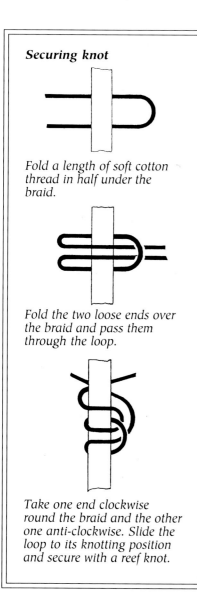

Securing knot

Fold a length of soft cotton thread in half under the braid.

Fold the two loose ends over the braid and pass them through the loop.

Take one end clockwise round the braid and the other one anti-clockwise. Slide the loop to its knotting position and secure with a reef knot.

3 Slide the weight bag down the braid on to the base of the marudai.

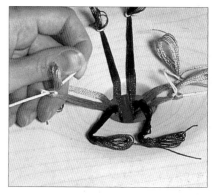

4 Pull the cotton leader on each attaching knot to release the leaders from the warp threads.

5 Finally, when all the bobbins have been removed, release the weight bag from the end of the braid. Both ends of the braid are secure, and you can now finish the ends with tassels (see overleaf).

Making tassels

There are countless designs of
fancy tassels and endings that
can be applied to braids.
However, as this book is just a
beginner's guide to braidmaking
only instructions for a basic
tassel have been included.

1 Thread a needle with a com-
patible thread and sew a
couple of stitches into the braid a
short distance from the end.

2 Wind the thread tightly round
the braid to make a neat length
of whipping. Secure the end with
a couple of small stitches.

Tip
Steam the braid over the
spout of a boiling kettle to
remove kinks and to
straighten out the tassel
threads.

3 Cut the threads at the blunt
end and tease them out with
your finger. Repeat stages 1 and 2
on the other end of the braid.

4 Roll a short strip of paper
round the tassel and trim off
the ends with a sharp pair of
scissors.

Opposite:
*The completed square braid together with variations made
using the same sequence of moves and with their contrasting
colours arranged in a similar manner round the marudai.*

Developing patterns

You can use the same sequence of four moves to create a whole host of different patterns: use more colours and change their starting positions on the marudai; use uneven numbers of threads on the bobbins; and introduce different textures.

Wind the individual bobbins as shown on pages 14–16 and set up the marudai using the warp detail diagrams. Make the braid using the sequence of moves given on pages 18–19.

Using different start positions

Below are the warp details for the four braids shown opposite, each of which have warp threads of the same thickness.

Warp details, braid 1
Bobbin weights: 70g (2½oz)
Weight bag: 250g (9oz)
● *Six strands, navy cotton pearl No 5*
◐ *Six strands, gold cotton pearl No 5*

Warp details, braid 2
Bobbin weights: 70g (2½oz)
Weight bag: 250g (9oz)
● *Six strands, navy cotton pearl No 5*
◐ *Six strands, gold cotton pearl No 5*
○ *Six strands, cream cotton pearl No 5*

Warp details, braid 3
Bobbin weights: 70g (2½oz)
Weight bag: 250g (9oz)
● *Six strands, navy cotton pearl No 5*
◐ *Six strands, gold cotton pearl No 5*
○ *Six strands, cream cotton pearl No 5*

Warp details, braid 4
Bobbin weights: 70g (2½oz)
Weight bag: 250g (9oz)
● *Six strands, navy cotton pearl No 5*
◐ *Six strands, gold cotton pearl No 5*
○ *Six strands, cream cotton pearl No 5*
● *Six strands, blue cotton pearl No 5*

By using more colours and by rearranging the start positions of the threads, other patterns can be achieved. From the left, braids 1, 2, 3 and 4.

Using uneven numbers of threads

By working with a different number of threads on each bobbin, the basic 'square' structure of the braid is distorted. The two braids on the left of the picture opposite (see warp details 5 and 6) are just two of the countless combinations that you can use to vary the look of a braid.

Warp details, braid 5
Bobbin weights: 100g (3½oz)
Weight bag: 300g (10½oz)
◎ Four strands, gold cotton pearl No 5
○ Sixteen strands, cream cotton pearl No 5

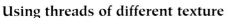

Warp details, braid 6
Bobbin weights: 100g (3½oz)
Weight bag: 300g (10½oz)
● Four strands, navy cotton pearl No 5
◉ Sixteen strands, blue cotton pearl No 5

Using threads of different texture

Working with threads of different texture or combinations of texture can create a completely new feel to the finished braid. The warp details for the two textured braids shown on the right of the picture opposite are given below.

Warp details, braid 7
Bobbin weights: 70g (2½oz)
Weight bag: 225g (8oz)
○ Eight strands, cream cotton pearl No 5
◎ Eight strands, ochre cotton bouclé

Warp details, braid 8
Bobbin weights: 70g (2½oz)
Weight bag: 225g (8oz)
◉ Six strands, blue cotton chenille
● Four strands, navy cotton pearl No 5

By using uneven numbers of threads on the bobbins and by introducing textured threads, all sorts of wonderful braids can be made. From the left, braids 5, 6, 7 and 8.

ROUND BRAID

By following a new sequence of moves, a tight, round braid with a spiral design can be made. In this project traditional Japanese braiding threads (biron or silk), which result in richer and sleeker braids, are used for the warp. These ropes save time and effort because the threads are already grouped as ready-to-use ropes.

Winding bobbins

Full-length biron ropes are 2.7m (9ft) long and make a 140cm (55in) braid plus tassels. This is quite a long length to produce, so you may wish to wind just half a length on each bobbin instead.

During the preparation of the warp, take care not to lose the natural twist on the ropes as this will help to distinguish one rope from another.

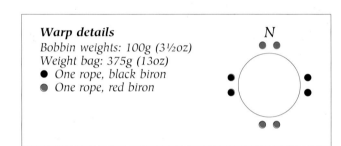

Warp details
Bobbin weights: 100g (3½oz)
Weight bag: 375g (13oz)
● *One rope, black biron*
◉ *One rope, red biron*

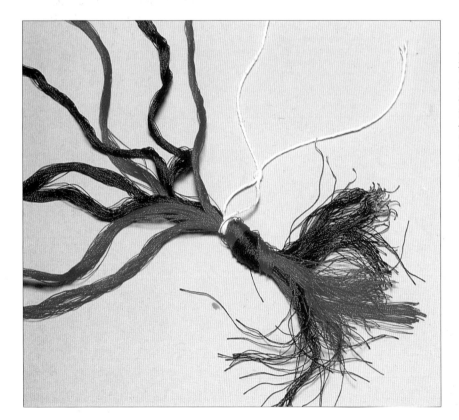

1 Take all eight ropes and, using the securing knot shown on page 21, tie all the ends together very tightly with soft cotton. To be really safe, tie an overhand knot on the end of the ropes to prevent the threads from slipping through your cotton tie. Next, create a loop in your cotton tie by tying another knot a short distance from the first.

2 Bring the warp threads to the marudai and insert the chopstick through the cotton loop, underneath the mirror.

3 Temporarily place the weight bag on some of the ropes to prevent the chopstick from falling out. Now peel away one biron rope.

4 Smooth the rope out, attach it to the bobbin leader as shown on page 15, roll it on to the bobbin and secure it with a slip knot (page 16). Repeat this with the other seven ropes.

5 Arrange the threads round the surface of the marudai. Place pairs of red ropes at the north and south positions and pairs of black ropes at the east and west positions.

Developing patterns

As with the square braid, you can create many new round braids by changing colours, start positions, numbers of threads and texture.

Using different start positions

Here is a selection of eight braids that can be created using the round braid sequence of moves. The warp details for each braid are shown below. They are all made using one rope of biron on each bobbin.

Warp details, braid 1
Bobbin weights: 100g (3½oz)
Weight bag: 375g (13oz)
● One rope, black biron
● One rope, green biron
◐ One rope, silver metallised biron

Warp details, braid 2
Bobbin weights: 100g (3½oz)
Weight bag: 375g (13oz)
● One rope, black biron
○ One rope, light-green biron

Warp details, braid 3
Bobbin weights: 100g (3½oz)
Weight bag: 375g (13oz)
● One rope, black biron
○ One rope, light-green biron
◐ One rope, silver metallised biron

Warp details, braid 4
Bobbin weights: 100g (3½oz)
Weight bag: 375g (13oz)
● One rope, green biron
○ One rope, light-green biron
◐ One rope, silver metallised biron

Warp details, braid 5
Bobbin weights: 100g (3½oz)
Weight bag: 375g (13oz)
● One rope, black biron
○ One rope, light-green biron

Warp details, braid 6
Bobbin weights: 100g (3½oz)
Weight bag: 375g (13oz)
● One rope, black biron
◐ One rope, silver metallised biron

Warp details, braid 7
Bobbin weights: 100g (3½oz)
Weight bag: 375g (13oz)
● One rope, black biron
● One rope, green biron
○ One rope, light-green biron

Warp details, braid 8
Bobbin weights: 100g (3½oz)
Weight bag: 375g (13oz)
● One rope, black biron
● One rope, green biron
○ One rope, light-green biron

Opposite:
These eight braids, all with different patterns, are made with one rope of biron on each bobbin.
From the left: braids 1, 2, 3, 4, 5, 6, 7 and 8.

Using uneven numbers of threads

The four braids at the top of the picture opposite are made using the warp details below. They are all made from the same type of silk thread but with a different number of threads wound on each bobbin.

Warp details, braid 1

Bobbin weights: 70g (2½oz)
Weight bag: 250g (9oz)
○ *Half rope (twenty strands), gold silk*
○ *Two ropes (eighty strands), yellow silk*

The appearance of the braid is improved by using an S-twist on the threads (see page 13). This braid uses uneven lengths of warp threads. If you make your own warp, wind 100cm (40in) of yellow to 80cm (32in) of gold.

Warp details, braid 2

Bobbin weights: 100g (3½oz)
Weight bag: 300g (10½oz)
○ *Half rope (twenty strands), white silk*
◉ *Three ropes (120 strands), gold silk*

The appearance of the braid is improved by using an S-twist on the threads (see page 13).

Warp details, braid 3

Bobbin weights: 70g (2½oz)
Weight bag: 250g (9oz)
○ *Half rope (twenty strands), cream silk*
○ *Two ropes (eighty strands), white silk*

The appearance of the braid is improved by using an S-twist on the threads (see page 13). This braid uses uneven lengths of warp threads. If you make your own warp, wind 100cm (40in) of white to 80cm (32in) of cream.

Warp details, braid 4

Bobbin weights: 100g (3½oz)
Weight bag: 300g (10½oz)
◉ *Half rope (twenty strands), gold silk*
○ *Two ropes (eighty strands), cream silk*
○ *Three ropes (120 strands), white silk*

The appearance of the braid is improved by using an S-twist on the threads (see page 13).

Opposite:
A selection of round braids showing some of the ways you can alter the shape of the finished braid by varying the number of threads wound on to the bobbins, and by incorporating texture.
From the top, down: braids 1, 2, 3 and 4.
From the bottom, left: braids 5, 6, 7 and 8.

Adding texture

You can change both the feel and look of a braid by using threads that have contrasting textures. Below are the warp details of the two braids at the bottom left of the picture opposite. These braids contain mohair and knitting yarn to contrast with silk. Some unusual effects can also be produced by incorporating machine-made braids and cords in the warp, and the braids shown at bottom right are made in this way.

Warp details, braid 5

Bobbin weights: 100g (3½oz)
Weight bag: 400g (14oz)
○ *Forty strands, white silk*
○ *Sixteen strands, white mohair*

This braid uses uneven lengths of warp threads. If you make your own warp, wind 100cm (40in) of mohair to 80cm (32in) of silk.

Warp details, braid 6

Bobbin weights: 100g (3½oz)
Weight bag: 400g (14oz)
◉ *Forty strands, gold silk*
● *Four strands, fancy knitting yarn*

This braid uses uneven lengths of warp threads. If you make your own warp, wind 100cm (40in) of fancy knitting yarn to 80cm (32in) of silk.

Warp details, braid 7

Bobbin weights: 100g (3½oz)
Weight bag: 250g (9oz)
◉ *One rope (forty strands), gold silk*
○ *One rope (thirty strands), gold metallised biron*
◉ *3mm (⅛in) wide, gold cotton/viscose Russia braid*
○ *3mm (⅛in) diameter, yellow viscose/acrylic lacing cord*

This braid uses uneven lengths of warp threads. If you make your own warp, wind 165cm (65in) of Russia braid to 100cm (40in) of the other threads.

Warp details, braid 8

Bobbin weights: 100g (3½oz)
Weight bag: 300g (10½oz)
○ *One rope (forty strands), white silk*
◉ *One rope (thirty strands), gold metallised biron*
○ *3mm (⅛in) wide, white cotton/viscose Russia braid*
○ *6mm (¼in) diameter, white cotton/acrylic crepe cord*

This braid uses uneven lengths of warp threads. If you make your own warp, wind 100cm (40in) of gold biron, 135cm (53in) of white silk, 140cm (55in) of crepe cord and 230cm (90in) of Russia braid.

FLAT BRAID

The following sequence of four moves produces a very
flat braid, with a distinct chevron design on one side
and a more broken design on the other. For this project
wind the warp using the method shown on pages 14–17.
A one metre (40in) warp will make a fine silk braid
about 55cm (22in) long, plus tassels.

Winding the warp

Prepare a warp as shown on
pages 14–17, winding four
bobbins with twenty strands of
green silk and four with twenty
strands of light-green silk.
Arrange the bobbins round the
marudai so that the four green
bobbins are in the south and the
four light-green bobbins in the
north. Note that there are no
bobbins in the east or west.

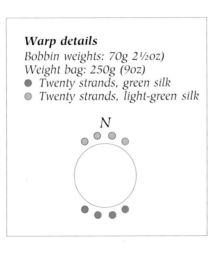

Warp details
Bobbin weights: 70g 2½oz)
Weight bag: 250g (9oz)
● *Twenty strands, green silk*
● *Twenty strands, light-green silk*

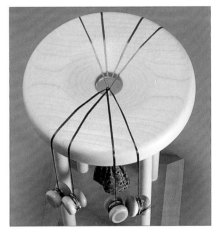

Working the braid

This type of flat braid is made
using a sequence of four basic
movements. The threads are
readjusted before the sequence
is repeated. For movement 4, the
bobbin in the right hand should
cross over the bobbin in the left
hand.

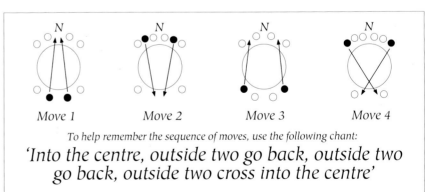

Move 1 *Move 2* *Move 3* *Move 4*

To help remember the sequence of moves, use the following chant:

'*Into the centre, outside two go back, outside two
go back, outside two cross into the centre*'

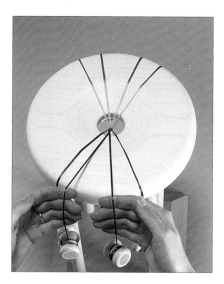

1 Lift the middle two threads at the south. . .

. . . and place them between the middle two threads at the north.

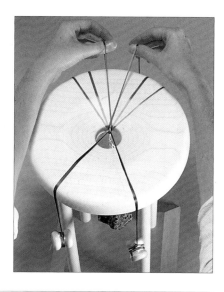

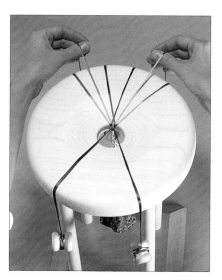

2 At the north, lift the two threads either side of the ones just placed down. . .

. . . and place them centrally at the south.

3 At the south, lift the threads either side of the ones just placed down. . .

. . . and place them at the north, between the outer and inner pairs of threads.

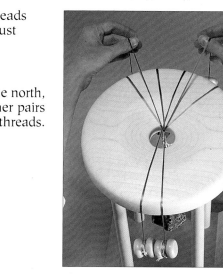

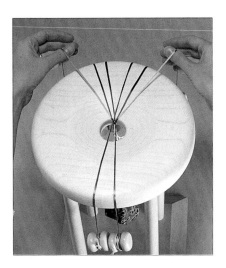

4 At the north, lift the two outermost threads. . .

. . . and place them at the south, **crossing** the right-hand thread over the left-hand one.

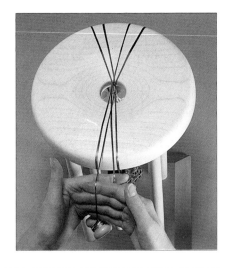

5 Re-adjust the positions of all the threads before repeating the sequence.

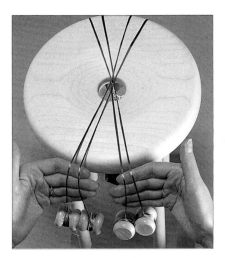

The two-tone green braid, together with a selection of similar braids in other colourways.

Points of braiding

The four points of braiding for this flat braid are shown here. Note the offset to the north at the start of move 2 and move 4. For this particular colour arrangement, the positions of the light- and dark-green threads will reverse after each set of moves.

Ready for the start of move 1. Braid in the middle of the hole.

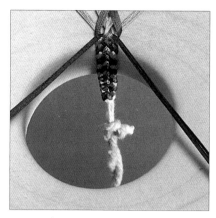

Ready to start move 2. Braid offset to the north.

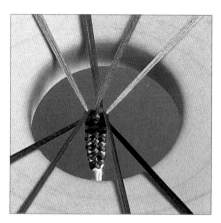

Ready to start move 3. Braid in the middle of the hole

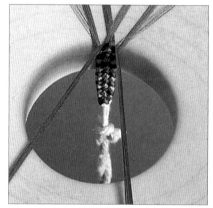

Ready to start move 4. Braid offset to the north.

Developing patterns

On these pages there are warp details for the eight braids shown. The four braids on the left are made using even numbers of threads on each bobbin, the next two are made using uneven numbers of threads, while the two on the right incorporate pre-made braids.

Using different start positions

Warp details, braid 1
Bobbin weights: 100g (3½oz)
Weight bag: 400g (14oz)
- One rope, black biron
- One rope, blue biron
- One rope, purple biron
- One rope, beige biron

Warp details, braid 2
Bobbin weights: 100g (3½oz)
Weight bag: 350g (12oz)
- One rope, blue biron
- One rope, beige biron

Warp details, braid 3
Bobbin weights: 100g (3½oz)
Weight bag: 350g (12oz)
- One rope, black biron
- One rope, petrol-blue biron
- One rope, purple biron

Warp details, braid 4
Bobbin weights: 100g (3½oz)
Weight bag: 400g (14oz)
- One rope, blue biron
- One rope, purple biron
- One rope, beige biron

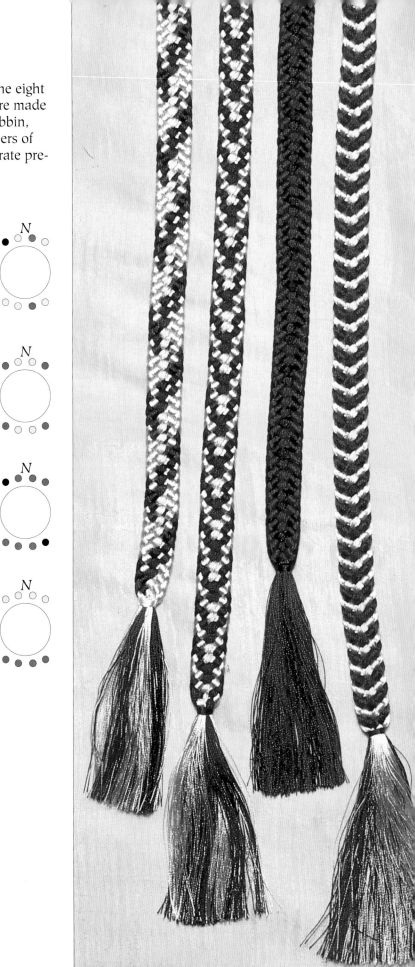

Using uneven numbers of threads

Warp details, braid 5
Bobbin weights: 70g (2½oz)
Weight bag: 200g (7oz)
● Half rope (twenty strands), blue biron
● Two ropes (eighty strands), purple biron

Warp details, braid 6
Bobbin weights: 70g (2½oz)
Weight bag: 200g (7oz)
● Half rope (twenty strands), petrol-blue biron
● Two ropes (eighty strands), purple biron

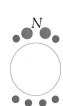

Adding texture

Warp details, braid 7
Bobbin weights: 100g (3½oz)
Weight bag: 400g (14oz)
○ One rope, beige silk
● Hollow braid (see pages 46–8 for the
sequence of moves):

Warp details, hollow braid
Bobbin weight: 100g (3½oz)
Weight bag: 300g (10½oz)
● One rope purple silk
● One rope petrol-blue silk

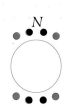

This braid uses uneven lengths of warp threads. If you make
your own warp, wind 100cm (40in) of beige to 75cm (30in)
of hollow braid.

Warp details, braid 8
Bobbin weights: 100g (3½oz)
Weight bag: 300g (10½oz)
● One rope, blue silk
● manufactured Kumihimo black silk cord,
1mm (0.04in) square

*A selection of the wonderful patterns that you can make
using the four move sequence for flat braids.
From the left: braids 1, 2, 3, 4, 5, 6, 7 and 8.*

HONEYCOMB BRAID

A sequence of six moves makes this textured round braid. It has large parallel stitches that create a honeycomb structure.

Winding the bobbins

Wind the bobbins with biron ropes using the method shown on pages 26–7, and arrange them round the marudai, with the blue threads at the north, south, east and west, and the light-blue threads at the north-east, south-east, south-west and north-west.

A full-length biron rope will make a 150cm (60in) length of braid with tassels at each end.

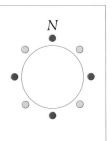

Warp details
Bobbin weights: 100g (3½oz)
Weight bag: 350g (12oz)
● *One rope, blue biron*
○ *One rope, light-blue biron*

The take up of the braid is uneven making about 30cm (12in) wastage on the light-blue ropes.

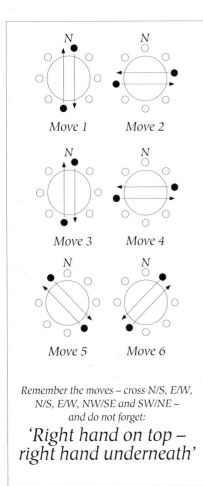

Move 1 Move 2

Move 3 Move 4

Move 5 Move 6

Remember the moves – cross N/S, E/W, N/S, E/W, NW/SE and SW/NE – and do not forget:

'Right hand on top – right hand underneath'

Working the braid

Each movement in the sequence is a straight swap of opposite threads, but the threads must be lifted with the correct hands so that they pass each other correctly. For moves 1, 3 and 5 the right hand must start at the top, and for moves 2, 4 and 6 the right hand must start underneath.

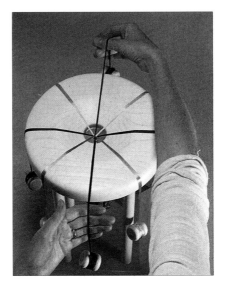

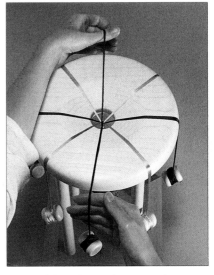

1 Lift the north threads with the right hand and the south threads with the left hand . . .

. . . and lay them down at the south and north respectively.

2 Lift the west threads with the right hand and the east threads with the left hand . . .

. . . and lay them down at the east and west respectively.

3 Lift the north threads with the right hand and the south threads with the left hand . . .

. . . and lay them down at the south and north respectively.

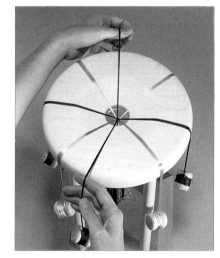

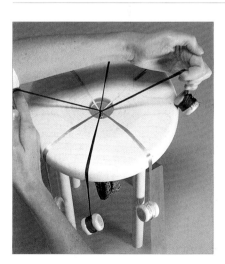

4 Lift the west threads with the right hand and the east threads with the left hand . . .

. . . and lay them down at the east and west respectively.

41

5 Lift the north-west threads with the right hand and the south-east threads with the left hand . . .

. . . and lay them down at the south-east and north-west respectively.

6 Lift the south-west threads with the right hand and the north-east threads with the left hand . . .

. . . and lay them down at the north-east and south-west respectively.

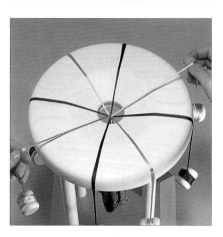

Points of braiding

Ready to start move 1.

Ready to start move 2.

Ready to start move 3.

Ready to start move 4.

Ready to start move 5.

Ready to start move 6.

*The finished braid, together with a selection
of braids made in different colourways.*

Developing patterns

A selection of honeycomb braids is shown on the page opposite. The four braids in the central knot are all made with the same number of threads on each bobbin. The top two braids are made with different thicknesses of threads, while those at the bottom are worked with ribbons and a variation of the basic sequence of moves.

Changing start positions

Warp details, braid 1
Bobbin weights: 100g (3½oz)
Weight bag: 350g (12oz)
○ One rope, beige biron
◉ One rope, pink biron
● One rope, burgundy biron

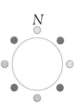

Warp details, braid 2
Bobbin weights: 100g (3½oz)
Weight bag: 350g (12oz)
○ One rope, light-pink biron
◉ One rope, pink biron

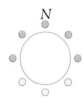

Warp details, braid 3
Bobbin weights: 100g (3½oz)
Weight bag: 350g (12oz)
○ One rope, beige biron
◉ One rope, pink biron
● One rope, burgundy biron

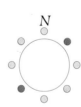

Warp details, braid 4
Bobbin weights: 100g (3½oz)
Weight bag: 350g (12oz)
○ One rope, light-pink biron
● One rope, burgundy biron

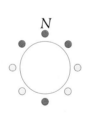

Working with different thicknesses

Warp details, braid 5
Bobbin weights: 100g (3½oz)
Weight bag: 300g (10½oz)
◉ Twenty strands, pink silk
○ Twelve strands, mauve linen

N

Warp details, braid 6
Bobbin weights: 100g (3½oz)
Weight bag: 300g (10½oz)
◉ Twenty strands, pink silk
○ Twelve strands, mauve linen

N

Note: The linen thread used for braids 5 and 6 is much heavier than the silk. It has a two-ply structure and weighs 330g/1000m (12oz/1000yd).

Changing the texture

Warp details, braid 7
Bobbin weights: 100g (3½oz)
Weight bag: 350g (12oz)
● Twenty strands, burgundy silk
◉ Picot-edged ribbon, 5mm (¼in) wide

This braid was improved by increasing the number of times the N/S, E/W threads were worked – here the sequence was 1, 2, 3, 4, 3, 4, 5, and 6.

Warp details, braid 8
Bobbin weights: 100g (3½oz)
Weight bag: 350g (12oz)
○ Twenty strands, light-pink silk
● Irridescent organdy ribbon, 15mm (½in) wide

N

This braid was improved by increasing the number of times the N/S, E/W threads were worked – here the sequence was 1, 2, 3, 4, 3, 4, 5, and 6.

Opposite:
From the top: braids 5 and 6;
braids 1, 4, 3 and 2;
and braids 7 and 8.

HOLLOW BRAID

A sequence of four moves is used to create this hollow round braid with a spotted design. The space inside the braid gives it a softness and flexibility that allows it to be formed into a flatter braid when squeezed.

Winding the bobbins

Biron ropes are used for this project (see pages 26–7). A full-length biron rope wound on each bobbin will make a braid approximately 150cm (60in) long.

Arrange the bobbins round the marudai as shown.

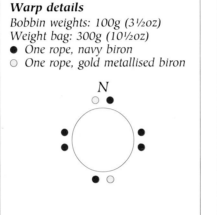

Warp details
Bobbin weights: 100g (3½oz)
Weight bag: 300g (10½oz)
● *One rope, navy biron*
○ *One rope, gold metallised biron*

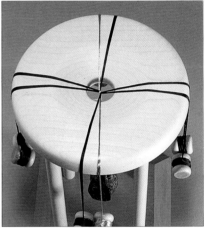

Working the braid

The sequence of moves needed to make this braid have a different 'feel' to previous sequences. For this braid, opposite sets of threads are lifted, and the moves rotate about the centre point. The first two moves are clockwise and the second two moves are anti-clockwise. When lifting the threads, it is important to use the correct hands as shown.

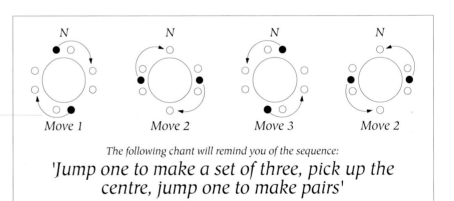

Move 1   *Move 2*   *Move 3*   *Move 2*

The following chant will remind you of the sequence:

'Jump one to make a set of three, pick up the centre, jump one to make pairs'

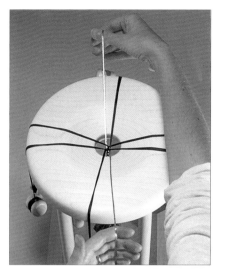

1 Lift the left-hand north and the right-hand south threads . . .

. . . rotate them clockwise, over one set of threads, and place them at top-east and bottom-west respectively.

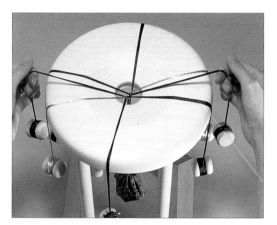

2 Lift the middle threads at the west and the east . . .

. . . rotate them clockwise, over one set of threads, and lay them down as left-hand north and right-hand south respectively.

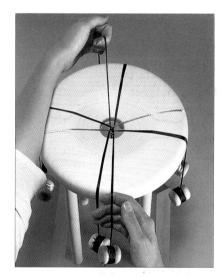

3 Lift right-hand north and left-hand south . . .

. . . rotate them anti-clockwise, over one set of threads, and lay them down at the top west and the bottom east respectively.

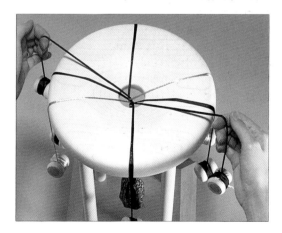

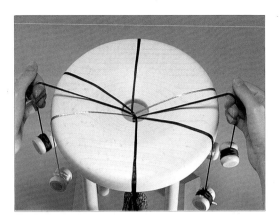

4 Lift the middle threads at the west and the east . . .

. . . rotate them anti-clockwise, over one set of threads, and lay them down at the right-hand north and the left-hand south respectively.

The finished braid, together with other effective colourways.

5 Before repeating the sequence of moves, readjust the threads so that they lie together in pairs.

Points of braiding

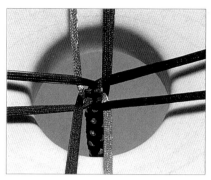

Ready to start move 1.

Ready to start move 2.

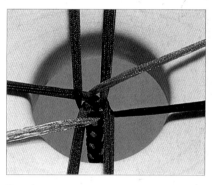

Ready to start move 3.

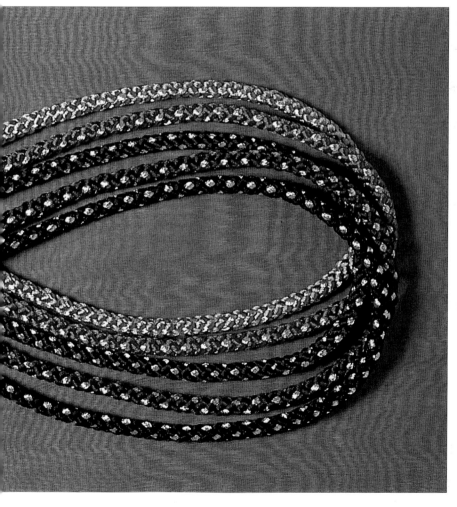

Ready to start move 4.

Developing patterns

Many combinations of colour and starting positions can be used to make hollow braids. Here are eight warp details for the braids shown opposite. They are all made using one rope of biron on each bobbin.

Warp details, braid 1
Bobbin weights: 100g (3½oz)
Weight bag: 300g (10½oz)
○ One rope, cream biron
● One rope, red biron
● One rope, black biron

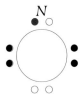

Warp details, braid 5
Bobbin weights: 100g (3½oz)
Weight bag: 300g (10½oz)
○ One rope, mauve biron
● One rope, black biron

Warp details, braid 2
Bobbin weights: 100g (3½oz)
Weight bag: 300g (10½oz)
○ One rope, mauve biron
○ One rope, grey biron
● One rope, black biron

Warp details, braid 6
Bobbin weights: 100g (3½oz)
Weight bag: 300g (10½oz)
○ One rope, mauve biron
● One rope, red biron
● One rope, black biron

Warp details, braid 3
Bobbin weights: 100g (3½oz)
Weight bag: 300g (10½oz)
● One rope, red biron
● One rope, black biron

Warp details, braid 7
Bobbin weights: 100g (3½oz)
Weight bag: 300g (10½oz)
○ One rope, cream biron
○ One rope, mauve biron
○ One rope, grey biron
● One rope, black biron

Warp details, braid 4
Bobbin weights: 100g (3½oz)
Weight bag: 300g (10½oz)
○ One rope, cream biron
○ One rope, mauve biron
○ One rope, grey biron
● One rope, black biron

Warp details, braid 8
Bobbin weights: 100g (3½oz)
Weight bag: 300g (10½oz)
● One rope, red biron
● One rope, black biron

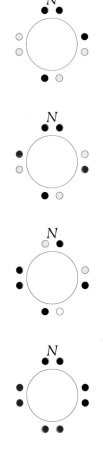

Opposite:
These braids were made with biron ropes, with a full length wound on to each bobbin. From the top tassel downwards: braids 1, 2, 4, 3, 6, 5, 8 and 7.

Working with different thicknesses

Warp details, braid 1
Bobbin weights: 70g (2½oz)
Weight bag: 250g (9oz)
◉ *Ten strands, pink silk*
○ *Eighty strands, pale-pink silk*

This braid was improved by adding a Z-twist (see page 13) to the pale-pink threads.

Warp details, braid 2
Bobbin weights: 100g (3½oz)
Weight bag: 350g (12oz)
◉ *Ten strands, bright-pink silk*
◉ *Eighty strands, turquoise silk*

This braid was improved by adding S- and Z-twists (see page 13) to the turquoise threads.

Warp details, braid 3
Bobbin weights: 70g (2½oz
Weight bag: 250g (9oz)
◉ *Ten strands, pink silk*
○ *Eighty strands, pale-pink silk*

This braid was improved by adding S- and Z-twists (see page 13) to the pale-pink threads.

Warp details, braid 4
Bobbin weights: 100g (3½oz)
Weight bag: 350g (12oz)
◉ *Twenty strands, bright-pink silk*
◉ *Twenty strands, blue silk*
● *Eighty strands, blue silk*
○ *Eighty strands, turquoise silk*

This braid was improved by adding S- and Z-twists (see page 13) to the threads as marked.

Changing texture

Warp details, braid 5
Bobbin weights: 70g (2½oz)
Weight bag: 200g (7oz)
○ *Twenty strands, turquoise silk*
● *3mm (⅛in) diameter, knitted viscose ribbon ruched on to an internal thread*

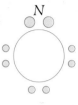

Warp details, braid 6
Bobbin weights: 70g (2½oz)
Weight bag: 200g (7oz)
○ *Twenty strands, turquoise silk*
◌ *Twenty strands, turquoise cotton bouclé*

Re-working braids

Warp details, braid 7
Bobbin weights: 70g (2½oz)
Weight bag: 225g (8oz)
● *Twenty strands, blue silk*
○ *Twenty strands, turquoise silk*
● *Twenty strands, black silk*
◉ *Round braid (see pages 26–9)*

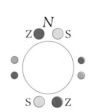

Warp details, round braid
Bobbin weight: 70g (2½oz)
Weight bag: 275g (10oz)
● *Twenty strands, red silk*
◌ *Twenty strands, pink silk*

The appearance of the braid was improved by putting an S-twist (see page 13) on the blue threads.

   This braid uses uneven lengths of warp threads. If you make your own warp, wind 100cm (40in) of turquoise to 100cm (40in) of blue, 90cm (36in) of black and 60cm (24in) of round braid.

Warp details, braid 8
Bobbin weights: 100g (3½oz)
Weight bag: 250g (9oz)
◉ *One rope pink biron*
◉ *One rope, bright-pink biron*
○ *3mm (⅛in) wide, pink cotton/viscose Russia braid*
○ *6mm (¼in) diameter, pink cotton/acrylic crepe cord*

This braid uses uneven lengths of warp threads. If you make your own warp, wind 100cm (40in) of bright-pink to 80cm (32in) of pink, 85cm (34in) of crepe cord and 140cm (55in) of Russia braid.

Opposite:
These hollow braids were made from the warp details shown on this page.
Top: braids 1, 2, 3 and 4.
Bottom left: braids 5 and 6.
Bottom right: braids 7 and 8.

ROUNDED FLAT BRAID

Compared with the really flat braid described on pages 34–39, this braid has a more rounded, fatter feel to it.

Winding the bobbins

For this project use twenty strands of silk on each bobbin, which should be wound as shown on page 14. A 100cm (40in) warp length will make a 60cm (24in) braid with tassels at each end. Arrange the threads round the marudai as shown.

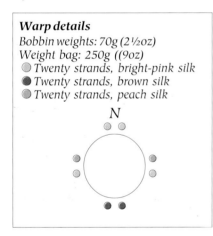

Warp details
Bobbin weights: 70g (2½oz)
Weight bag: 250g ((9oz)
  ○ *Twenty strands, bright-pink silk*
  ● *Twenty strands, brown silk*
  ○ *Twenty strands, peach silk*

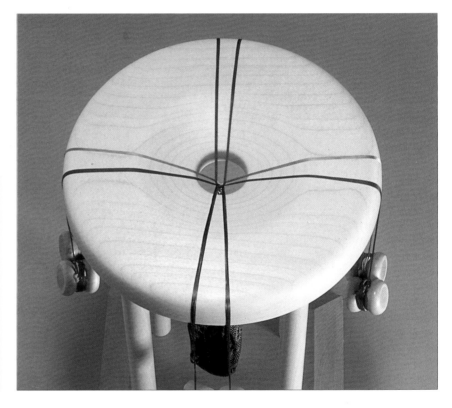

Working the braid

The first two moves in this sequence involve crossing the threads; it is essential that the correct hands are used when lifting them.

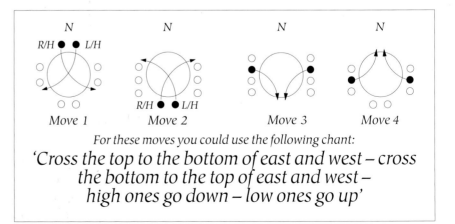

Move 1   Move 2   Move 3   Move 4

For these moves you could use the following chant:
'Cross the top to the bottom of east and west – cross the bottom to the top of east and west – high ones go down – low ones go up'

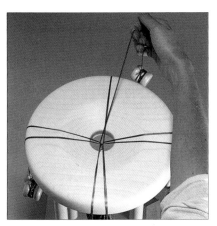

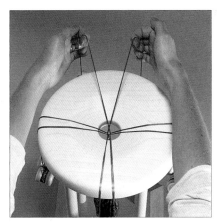

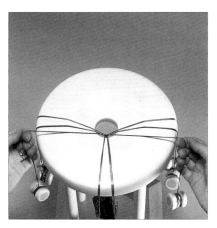

1 With the right hand, lift the left-hand north threads and cross them over the right-hand threads . . .

. . . still holding the first threads in the right hand, lift the other set of threads with the left hand . . .

. . . and lay both sets of threads down below the pairs of threads at the west and east.

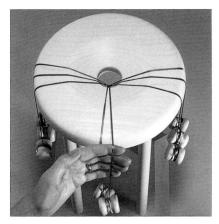

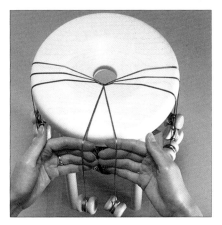

2 With the left hand, lift the right-hand south threads and cross them over the left-hand threads . . .

. . . still holding the first threads in the left hand, lift the other set of threads with the right hand . . .

. . . and lay both sets of threads down above the groups of threads at the west and east.

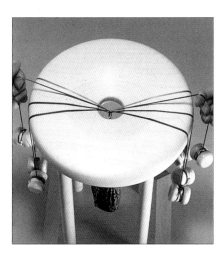

3 Lift the second-from-the-top set of threads at the west and east . . .

. . . and, without crossing them, lay them down at the south.

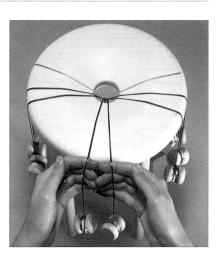

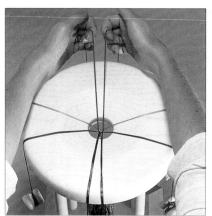

4 Lift the middle set of threads at the west and east . . .

. . . and, without crossing them, lay them down at the north.

Finally, readjust the warps at the north and south and then at the east and west.

Points of braiding

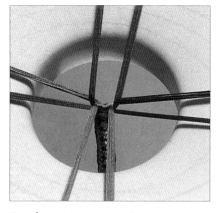

Ready to start move 1.

Ready to start move 2. The uneven distribution of the bobbins offsets the point of braiding to the south.

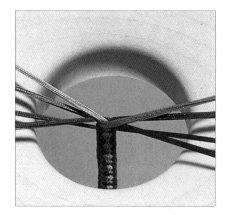

Ready to start move 3.

Ready to start move 4. Again, the uneven distribution of the bobbins offsets the point of braiding to the south.

The finished braid, together with a selection of braids in different colourways. The braids are small, but the enlargement above clearly shows the lovely patterning.

Developing patterns

There are hundreds of combinations of both colourways and distribution of colour that can be used with this braid. Below are the warp details for the eight braids shown opposite. These were made with one rope of biron wound on each bobbin. On the following pages are details for other variations .

Warp details, braid 1
Bobbin weights: 100g (3½oz)
Weight bag: 300g (10½oz)
● One rope, blue biron
● One rope, purple biron
○ One rope, gold metallised biron

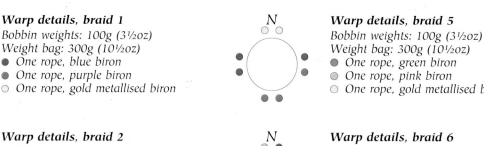

Warp details, braid 2
Bobbin weights: 100g (3½oz)
Weight bag: 300g (10½oz)
○ One rope, pink biron
● One rope, blue biron

Warp details, braid 3
Bobbin weights: 100g (3½oz)
Weight bag: 300g (10½oz)
● One rope, green biron
● One rope, blue biron
○ One rope, pink biron

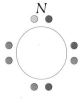

Warp details, braid 4
Bobbin weights: 100g (3½oz)
Weight bag: 300g (10½oz)
● One rope, blue biron
○ One rope, gold metallised biron

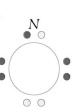

Warp details, braid 5
Bobbin weights: 100g (3½oz)
Weight bag: 300g (10½oz)
● One rope, green biron
○ One rope, pink biron
○ One rope, gold metallised biron

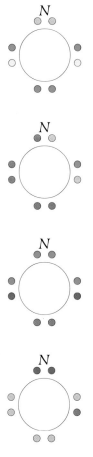

Warp details, braid 6
Bobbin weights: 100g (3½oz)
Weight bag: 300g (10½oz)
● One rope, green biron
○ One rope, pink biron
● One rope, purple biron

Warp details, braid 7
Bobbin weights: 100g (3½oz)
Weight bag: 300g (10½oz)
● One rope, green biron
● One rope, blue biron
● One rope, purple biron

Warp details, braid 8
Bobbin weights: 100g (3½oz)
Weight bag: 300g (10½oz)
○ One rope, pink biron
● One rope, blue biron
● One rope, purple biron

Opposite:
All these rounded flat braids were made using
a single rope of biron on each bobbin.
From the left: braids 1, 2, 3, 4, 5, 6, 7 and 8.

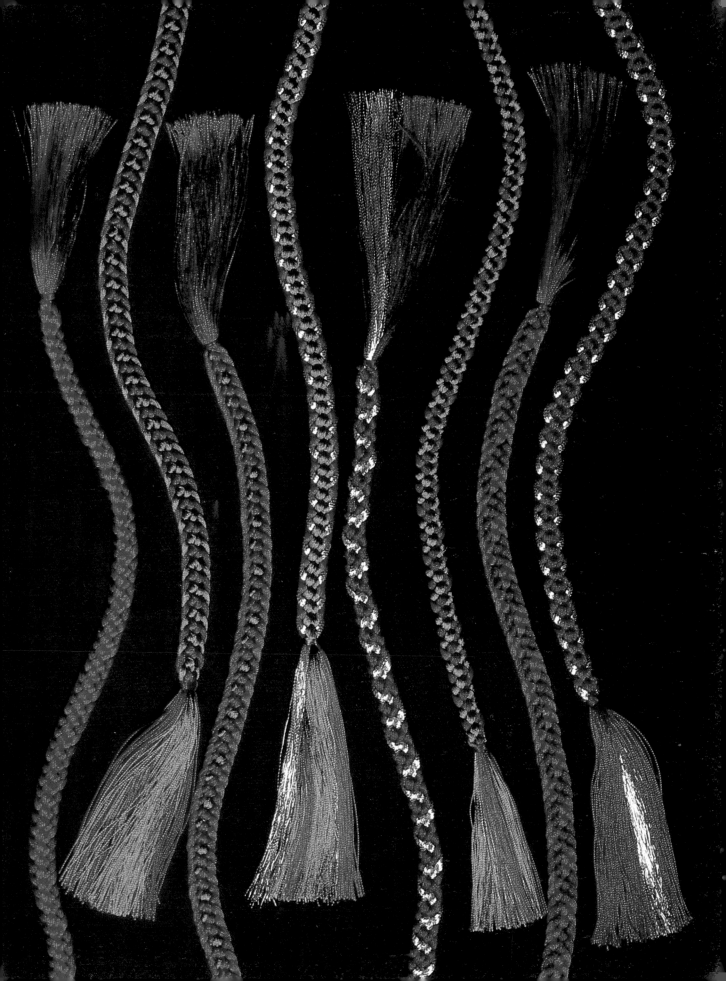

Working with different thicknesses

Warp details, braid 1
Bobbin weights: 100g (3½oz)
Weight bag: 300g (10½oz)
○ *Half rope (twenty strands), yellow silk*
● *Two ropes (eighty strands), purple silk*

Warp details, braid 2
Bobbin weights: 100g (3½oz)
Weight bag: 300g (10½oz)
● *Half rope (twenty strands), orange silk*
● *Half rope (twenty strands), red silk*
● *Two ropes (eighty strands), black silk*

Warp details, braid 3
Bobbin weights: 100g (3½oz)
Weight bag: 300g (10½oz)
● *Half rope (twenty strands), black silk*
● *Two ropes (eighty strands), fancy dyed silk*

Warp details, braid 4
Bobbin weights: 100g (3½oz)
Weight bag: 300g (10½oz)
○ *Half rope (twenty strands), yellow silk*
● *Two ropes (eighty strands), purple silk*

Re-working braids

Warp details, braid 5
Bobbin weights: 100g (3½oz)
Weight bag: 300g (10½oz)
● *One rope, black biron*
● *One rope, red biron*
○ *3mm (⅛in) wide, black cotton/viscose Russia braid*
● *6mm (¼in) diameter, black cotton/acrylic crepe cord*

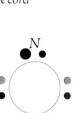

Warp details, braid 6
Bobbin weights: 100g (3½oz)
Weight bag: 400g (14oz)
● *One rope, black biron*
● *One rope, red biron*
● *One rope, orange biron*
● *6mm (¼in) diameter, black cotton/acrylic crepe cord*

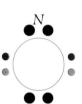

Warp details, braid 7
Bobbin weights: 100g (3½oz)
Weight bag: 300g (10½oz)
● *One rope, orange silk*
● *One rope, red silk*
● *Six strands, black cotton chenille*

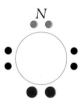

Warp details, braid 8
Bobbin weights: 100g (3½oz)
Weight bag: 325g (11½oz)
● *Two ropes (eighty strands), purple silk*
● *Two ropes (eighty strands), black silk*
● *3mm (⅛in) diameter, knitted viscose ribbon, ruched on to an internal thread*

Opposite:
You can create some really stunning braids with the sequence of moves shown on pages 56–8, by using uneven numbers of threads on each bobbin, and by re-working braids.
From the top: braids 1, 2, 3, 4, 5, 6, 7 and 8.

USING YOUR BRAIDS

Intricately woven silken braids and tassels can be used to complement all kinds of accessories, soft furnishings, clothing and textiles. Colours and textures can be mixed and matched to create a stylish and unique finish to curtains, cushions, bags and many more items; special finishing techniques can add individuality to a plain or patterned background.

You have already been shown how to alter colours, threads and textures. Now you can try out the techniques to create your own projects, or adapt the ideas to match your colour schemes and decor. Here are just a few applications – develop your ideas and you will be able to create beautiful and practical items for yourself and your home.

The warm deep red of the smooth velvet curtain is complemented by this richly textured cream and gold hollow braid. There are many decorative possibilities for the application of braids on soft furnishings – tie-backs, edgings for window blinds, wall-hangings and cushions, textured designs and patterns on embroidered, appliqued and patchworked items, embellishments for furniture fabric – and more.

Beautiful decorative braids add a touch of glamour to a pair of glasses. Colours can be chosen to complement the frames – and matching braids can be used to decorate an embroidered glasses' case.

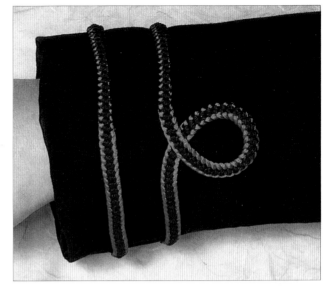

A rounded flat braid, couched on to the sleeves of a jacket, provides the perfect finishing touch. Fine silks can be braided with ribbons or metallic threads and couched on to collars and necklines, with matching accessories decorated with complementary colours in the same way.

These round braids are finished off with clasps and worn as eye-catching bracelets. Longer braids made in the same style could be used to make matching necklaces.

Square braids add a touch of elegance and style to these delicate silk bags. You could use any of the braids shown in this book to adorn fabric bags, which could be decorated with looped, woven or twisted designs, tassels and edgings.

Decorative braids add a personal finishing touch to a favourite photograph. This flat braid is made to measure, so that the delicate cream tassels lie either side of the oval edging.

INDEX